Lerner SPORTS

SUPER SPORTS
TEAMS

INSIDE THE
NEW YORK
YANKEES

JON M. FISHMAN

Lerner Publications ◆ Minneapolis

SPORTS THRILLS MEET RESEARCH SKILLS

Lerner SPORTS

Free Database Trial: **lernersports.com**

Lerner Publications Company
An imprint of Lerner Publishing Group, Inc.
241 First Avenue North
Minneapolis, MN 55401 USA

For reading levels and more information, look up this title at www.lernerbooks.com.

Main body text set in Aptifer Slab LT Pro / Typeface provided by Linotype AG

Designer: Kimberly Morales
Lerner team: Sue Marquis

Library of Congress Cataloging-in-Publication Data

Names: Fishman, Jon M., author.
Title: Inside the New York Yankees / Jon M. Fishman.
Description: Minneapolis : Lerner Publications, [2022] | Series: Super sports teams | Includes bibliographical
    references and index. | Audience: Ages 7–11 | Audience: Grades 2–3 | Summary: "The New York Yankees have
    dominated Major League Baseball with 27 World Series titles. From Babe Ruth to Aaron Judge, discover the
    superstars and iconic moments that put this team on top"—Provided by publisher.
Identifiers: LCCN 2021014945 (print) | LCCN 2021014946 (ebook) | ISBN 9781728441719 (library binding) |
    ISBN 9781728449470 (paperback) | ISBN 9781728445205 (ebook)
Subjects: LCSH: New York Yankees (Baseball team)—Juvenile literature.
Classification: LCC GV875.N4 F47 2022 (print) | LCC GV875.N4 (ebook) | DDC 796.357/64097471—dc23

LC record available at https://lccn.loc.gov/2021014945
LC ebook record available at https://lccn.loc.gov/2021014946

Manufactured in the United States of America
1-49926-49769-7/12/2021

TABLE OF CONTENTS

Hideki Matsui blasts the ball during the 2009 World Series.

BASEBALL'S BEST

FACTS AT A GLANCE

- From 1903 to 1913, **THE YANKEES** were called the Highlanders.

- In 1920, **BABE RUTH** hit more home runs than most Major League Baseball (MLB) teams hit.

- In 1956, **DON LARSEN** became the only pitcher to throw a perfect game in the World Series.

- **THE YANKEES** have more World Series wins, 27, than any other team has.

The New York Yankees faced the Philadelphia Phillies in the 2009 World Series. The Phillies won the first game 6–1. The Yankees rallied and won three of the next four games.

The teams played Game 6 on a cold November night in New York. In the second inning, New York's Hideki Matsui faced pitching legend Pedro Martinez. On the eighth pitch of the at bat, Matsui crushed the ball. It sailed high over the right-field wall for a two-run home run.

Matsui faced Martinez again in the next inning with the bases loaded. He smacked a single to score two runs and put New York ahead 4–1. Matsui ended the game with six RBIs, tying a World Series record. Derek Jeter smacked three hits and scored two runs in the game for New York.

In the eighth inning, Mariano Rivera pitched for the Yankees. MLB's best closer got the final five outs for the team. New York won 7–3. The Yankees were World Series champions!

The league's top teams have all won the World Series. But championship trophies and victory parades are common for the Yankees and their fans. The 2009 win was the 27th World Series title for New York. No other team has won half as many World Series.

The Yankees are one of the most valuable sports teams in the world. But when they started, they weren't called the Yankees. For their first two seasons, they didn't even play in New York City.

Rivera throws a pitch during Game 6 of the 2009 World Series.

The Yankees celebrate winning their 27th World Series title.

Babe Ruth keeps his eyes on the ball during batting practice in 1927. Many fans consider Ruth to be the first Yankees superstar.

THE TEAM THAT RUTH BUILT

The 1901 Baltimore Orioles were an average team. They finished their first season in MLB's American League (AL) in fifth place out of eight teams. In 1902, they finished last in the AL.

In January 1903, Frank Farrell and Bill Devery bought the Orioles for $18,000. Farrell and Devery planned to move the team from Baltimore, Maryland, to New York City. But first, they had to build a ballpark before the season started in April.

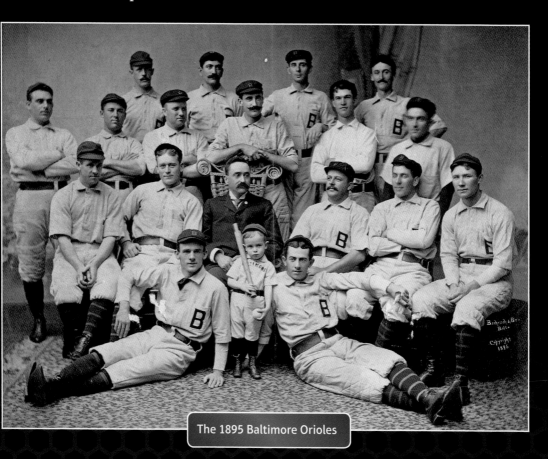

The 1895 Baltimore Orioles

Work began on a rocky hilltop in Manhattan, one of New York City's five boroughs. The new field became Hilltop Park, and the Baltimore Orioles became the New York Highlanders. The Highlanders played their first game on April 22, 1903. They lost to the Washington Senators 3–1.

The Highlanders won their first game the next day and finished the season with a winning record. The team had settled into its new home. But the name Highlanders was long and hard to fit into newspaper stories. Reporters began calling them the Yankees.

In 1912, the Highlanders moved to another stadium in Manhattan. They shared the Polo Grounds with the National League's (NL) New York Giants. The Highlanders formally changed their name to the Yankees in 1913.

The New York Highlanders playing at Hilltop Park

The Highlanders before playing on opening day of the 1908 season

Soon the Yankees made another move that would change the team forever. Babe Ruth helped the Boston Red Sox win three World Series from 1915 to 1918. In 1920, the Yankees paid the Red Sox $125,000 for Ruth to join their team.

Ruth focused on pitching with Boston. But in his final year with the team, he began batting more often. His 29 home runs in 1919 were by far the most in MLB. The Yankees wanted Ruth to focus on hitting. The results shocked the baseball world.

Ruth hit 665 career home runs for the Yankees.

In 1920, Ruth smashed 54 home runs. No one in MLB had ever come close to hitting that many big flies in a season. The player who finished second that year, George Sisler, hit 19 home runs. Ruth hit more homers alone than almost every other MLB team hit.

The next year, Ruth broke his own record with 59 home runs. In 1927, he smacked 60 big flies. His record stood for almost 35 years.

Ruth's home runs helped the Yankees win. They made it to the World Series in 1921 and 1922. Both years, the Yankees lost to the Giants. In 1923, the Yankees left the Polo Grounds. Their new home, Yankee Stadium, opened in the Bronx. Reporters called it the House That Ruth Built. The Yankees won their first World Series that year.

Ruth played his last game for the Yankees in 1934. He had helped New York win four World Series titles. No one could replace him, but the team kept up its winning ways. Ruth had set the Yankees on a path to become MLB's greatest team.

Yankees players celebrate winning the 1962 World Series.

Aaron Judge has had a lot of amazing moments with the Yankees.

AMAZING MOMENTS

Yankees history is full of great moments. One of the earliest took place on the first day of the 1923 season. Yankee Stadium was brand new, and fans were excited. At the time, the crowd of 74,000 was the biggest in MLB history. The Yankees led the Red Sox 1–0 in the third inning. Ruth batted with two runners on base. He smashed the ball for a home run, his first in the House That Ruth Built. He waved his hat to the cheering crowd as he ran around the bases. New York won 4–1.

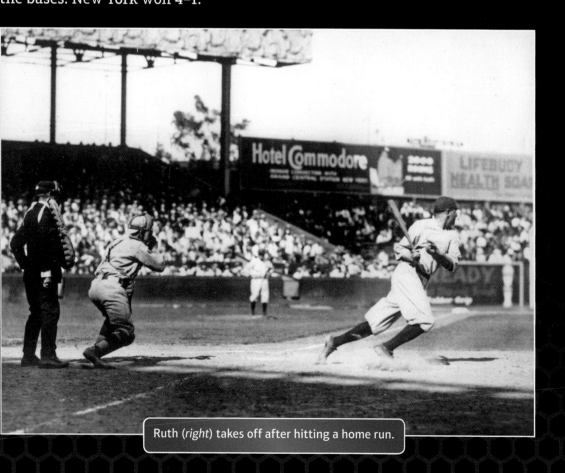

Ruth (*right*) takes off after hitting a home run.

In 1941, Joe DiMaggio thrilled Yankees fans with a hitting display of his own. On May 15, he struck a single against the Chicago White Sox. For the next two months, he got at least one hit in every game he played.

DiMaggio kept hitting. His streak had reached an incredible 56 games. It finally ended on July 17 in a game against the Cleveland Indians. DiMaggio's hitting streak was 11 games longer than any other in MLB history.

DiMaggio hits a single in 1941.

In 1956, the Yankees won the AL for the 22nd time. Pitcher Don Larsen faced the Brooklyn Dodgers in Game 5 of the World Series. Inning after inning, the Dodgers failed to get a runner on base.

By the ninth, Larsen still hadn't allowed a base runner. He got two outs, then struck out Dale Mitchell to end the game. The Yankees won 2–0. Larsen is the only pitcher to throw a perfect game in the World Series.

In 1977, the Los Angeles Dodgers led by one run in Game 6 of the World Series. Yankees outfielder Reggie

YANKEES FACT

In 1961, Yankees outfielder Roger Maris hit 61 home runs in 161 games. He beat Babe Ruth's home run record on the last day of the season.

Jackson came to bat in the fourth inning. He didn't waste any time. Jackson blasted a home run on the first pitch he saw. He did the same in the fifth and eighth innings. The Yankees won the game and the World Series. Since the game took place in October, Jackson earned the nickname Mr. October.

New York had a new home run record breaker in 2017. In a September game, outfielder Aaron Judge blasted his 49th and 50th big flies of the year. He set a new home run record for first-year players. Every season, the Yankees add more memorable moments that thrill fans.

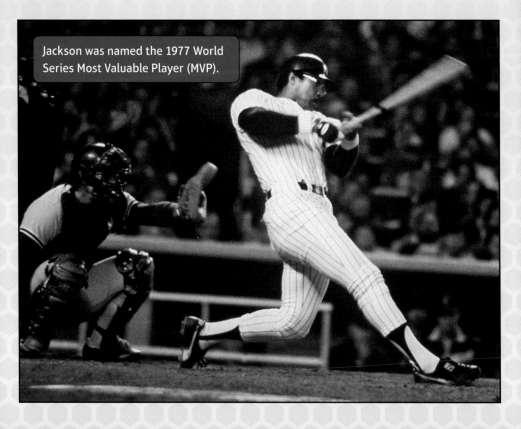

Jackson was named the 1977 World Series Most Valuable Player (MVP).

Yankees outfielder Bernie Williams helped the team win the World Series four times: 1996, 1998, 1999, and 2000.

YANKEES SUPERSTARS

The Yankees have had far too many amazing players to cover them all. Babe Ruth's stats could fill a book. After Ruth left, Lou Gehrig and Joe DiMaggio became the team's star players. With Gehrig and DiMaggio leading the way, the Yankees won the World Series four years in a row from 1936 to 1939.

New York soon had another winning streak. From 1949 to 1953, the Yankees were World Series champions each year. Catcher Yogi Berra won three AL MVP awards. The Yankees won an amazing 10 World Series titles with Berra.

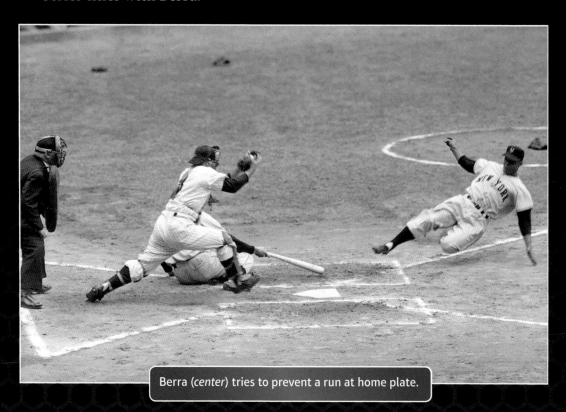

Berra (*center*) tries to prevent a run at home plate.

In 1951, Mickey Mantle joined the Yankees at just 19 years old. He didn't play much at first. But by the mid-1950s, he was the best hitter in the AL. In 1956, Mantle led the AL in batting average, home runs, and RBIs. He was the first Yankee to lead the league in all three stats since Gehrig did it in 1934.

Reggie Jackson helped the Yankees win the World Series in 1977 and 1978. But then almost 20 years passed without a championship in the Bronx. That streak ended in 1996 when Derek Jeter, Bernie

Mantle hit 52 home runs in 1956.

Derek Jeter (*second from left*) and teammates hug and cheer after winning the 1996 World Series.

Williams, and Andy Pettitte led New York to the title. Beginning in 1998, the team won the World Series three years in a row.

New superstars are always stepping up for the Yankees. Aaron Judge joined New York in 2017. A year later, the team added Giancarlo Stanton. Stanton was one of the strongest sluggers in the game.

Gerrit Cole led the Yankees in wins, strikeouts, and innings pitched in 2020.

Stanton proved his strength by blasting 38 home runs with 100 RBIs in his first season in New York. In 2020, the Yankees brought in Gerrit Cole. The pitching superstar wowed fans by striking out 94 batters in just 73 innings.

Stanton runs to catch a fly ball.

The outside of the current Yankee Stadium looks like the one that opened in 1923.

MONUMENT TO GREATNESS

In 1932, the Yankees honored former manager Miller Huggins with a monument at Yankee Stadium. The team later added monuments for Babe Ruth, Lou Gehrig, and others. The stones stood on the field just inside the center-field wall.

By the early 1970s, Yankee Stadium was almost 50 years old. New team owner George Steinbrenner began a two-year project to renew the building. In 1974 and 1975, the team played at Shea Stadium, where the New York Mets played. Yankee Stadium reopened in 1976 with many changes. One of the biggest was Monument Park. The team had moved their monuments to a special area behind the outfield wall.

Ruth (*left*), Huggins (*center*), and Gehrig sit together before a game in 1927.

In 2009, the team opened a brand-new Yankee Stadium. The $1.6 billion structure was designed to look like the old Yankee Stadium. The building was packed with modern features. And beyond the left-field wall stood Monument Park.

The Yankees are by far the most valuable baseball team in the world. No other MLB team comes close to matching their history of success. They haven't won the World Series since 2009. But superstars such as Aaron Judge, Giancarlo Stanton, and Gerrit Cole make the Yankees a powerful force in the AL. Someday soon they'll compete for the team's 28th World Series victory.

The new Monument Park features Yankees superstars who have had their jersey numbers retired.

Yankee Stadium seats 46,537 fans.

Mariano Rivera

YANKEES
SEASON RECORD
HOLDERS

HITS

1. Don Mattingly, 238 (1986)
2. Earle Combs, 231 (1927)
3. Lou Gehrig, 220 (1930)
4. Derek Jeter, 219 (1999)
5. Lou Gehrig, 218 (1927)

HOME RUNS

1. Roger Maris, 61 (1961)
2. Babe Ruth, 60 (1927)
3. Babe Ruth, 59 (1921)
4. Mickey Mantle, 54 (1961)
   Alex Rodriguez, 54 (2007)
   Babe Ruth, 54 (1920, 1928)

STOLEN BASES

1. Rickey Henderson, 93 (1988)
2. Rickey Henderson, 87 (1986)
3. Rickey Henderson, 80 (1985)
4. Fritz Maisel, 74 (1914)
5. Ben Chapman, 61 (1931)

WINS

1. Jack Chesbro, 41 (1904)
2. Carl Mays, 27 (1921)
   Al Orth, 27 (1906)
4. Bullet Joe Bush, 26 (1922)
   Russ Ford, 26 (1910)
   Lefty Gomez, 26 (1934)
   Carl Mays, 26 (1920)

STRIKEOUTS

1. Ron Guidry, 248 (1978)
2. Jack Chesbro, 239 (1904)
3. CC Sabathia, 230 (2011)
   Luis Severino, 230 (2017)
5. David Cone, 222 (1997)

SAVES

1. Mariano Rivera, 53 (2004)
2. Mariano Rivera, 50 (2001)
3. Dave Righetti, 46 (1986)
4. Mariano Rivera, 45 (1999)
5. Mariano Rivera, 44
   (2009, 2011, 2013)

GLOSSARY

batting average: the ratio of a batter's hits per times at bat

big fly: a home run

borough: one of the five divisions of New York City: Brooklyn, the Bronx, Manhattan, Queens, and Staten Island

closer: a relief pitcher who usually finishes games

home run: a hit that allows the player to circle all the bases in one play to score a run

manager: a person who directs a team

monument: a building, stone, or statue made to keep alive the memory of a person or event

perfect game: when a pitcher completes a game without allowing a base runner

rally: to come back from a low point

RBI: a run in baseball that is driven in by a batter

single: a hit that allows the batter to reach first base

LEARN MORE

Fishman, Jon M. *Baseball's G.O.A.T.: Babe Ruth, Mike Trout, and More*. Minneapolis: Lerner Publications, 2020.

Hewson, Anthony K. *Aaron Judge*. Minnetonka, MN: Kaleidoscope, 2019.

Levit, Joe. *Babe Ruth: Super Slugger*. Minneapolis: Lerner Publications, 2021.

New York Yankees
https://www.mlb.com/yankees

Sports Illustrated Kids—Baseball
https://www.sikids.com/baseball

Yankees Timeline
https://www.mlb.com/yankees/history/timeline-1900s

INDEX

PHOTO ACKNOWLEDGMENTS

Image credits: AP Photo/Elise Amendola, pp. 4, 7; AP Photo/Kathy Willens, p. 6; Bettmann/Getty Images, p. 8; Library of Congress/Corbis/VCG/Getty Images, p. 9; Mark Rucker/Transcendental Graphics/Getty Images, p. 10; Glasshouse Images/Alamy Stock Photo, p. 11; Bettmann/Getty Images, p. 12; AP Photo, pp. 13, 16, 17, 18, 19; AP Photo/Icon Sportswire, pp. 14, 23; Transcendental Graphics/Getty Images, p. 15; Stanley Weston/Getty Images, p. 20; Rich Pilling/MLB/Getty Images, p. 21; AP Photo/Frank Franklin II, p. 22; Mark Bonifacio/NY Daily News Archive/Getty Images, p. 24; Transcendental Graphics/Getty Images, p. 25; Jim McIsaac/Getty Images, p. 26; AP Photo/Seth Wenig, p. 27; AP Photo/Tammy Lechner, p. 28.

Design element: Master3D/Shutterstock.com.

Cover image: New York Daily News Archive/Getty Images.